Rooted

prayer journal

Copyright © 2021 by Stacy Filipkowski
All rights reserved.

For I know the plans I have for you," declares the Lord, "plans to prosper you and not to harm you, plans to give you hope and a future.

Jeremiah 29:11

This Rooted prayer Journal Belongs to:

Rooted
Prayer Journal

Find the adventure in following Jesus!

My command is this: Love each other as I have loved you.
// John 15:12

Introduction

Do you ever find yourself wondering why it seems difficult to hear from God? You pray earnestly, yet His presence feels distant, almost unreachable. Perhaps you know someone who appears to have an effortless connection with Him, confidently navigating the path He has laid out for them. How do they possess such unwavering certainty? Could it be that God has provided them with a personalized roadmap?

Over time, many individuals have shared with me a common sentiment: "I wish I could experience God's voice as clearly as you do. I long for that undeniable connection." The essence of this book/journal is to offer insights into this very topic and help you dismantle any barriers that may be hindering your journey toward a profound relationship with God—both in this life and beyond. It's a call to be intentional and to discover the thrill of following Jesus!

Important Events

MONTH   **YEAR**

Sunday	Monday	Tuesday	Wednesday	Thursday	Friday	Saturday

MY NOTES

MY NOTES

MY NOTES

Don't worry about anything; instead, pray about everything.
// Philippians 4:6

Prayer Wall Introduction

Welcome to your personal prayer wall—an intentional space for your prayer life. In our fast-paced world, it's easy to promise prayers during a chat or while scrolling through social media, only to forget later. It's human nature, and there's no shame in it. But imagine the impact of truly praying for each person you promised to. This section is designed to help you keep track of those in need of prayer, your own prayer requests, and to note when and how God answers these prayers.

Keeping track of your prayers serves a powerful purpose. It not only ensures you remember to pray for each request but also allows you to witness the beautiful ways God works in our lives. Often, we pray and move on, potentially missing the moment when our prayers are answered. By recording your prayers and their outcomes, you create a tangible record of faith in action, encouraging gratitude and strengthening your trust in God's timing and wisdom.

My Prayer Wall
"Prayer is Adventurous"

For Others:

[Y] Answered [N]

How has God answered or shifted this prayer?

For Myself:

[Y] Answered [N]

How has God answered or shifted this prayer?

My Prayer Wall
"Prayer is Adventurous"

For Others:

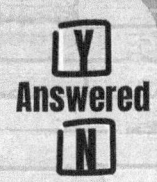

Answered: [Y] [N]

How has God answered or shifted this prayer?

For Myself:

Answered: [Y] [N]

How has God answered or shifted this prayer?

My Prayer Wall
"Prayer is Adventurous"

For Others:

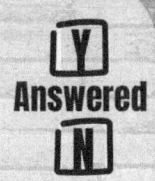

[Y] Answered [N]

How has God answered or shifted this prayer?

For Myself:

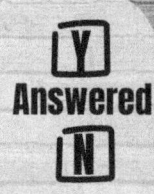

[Y] Answered [N]

How has God answered or shifted this prayer?

Prayer Challenges

Challenge 1 - Secret Prayer

Secret Prayer :

Have you ever wondered about the impact of silently praying for someone every day for 30 days? In this section, I encourage you to intercede for a person for an entire month and observe the transformative effects in their life. After the 30 days have concluded, the decision to reveal to them that you have been praying on their behalf is entirely yours. Alternatively, you may opt to keep this act of prayer a confidential bond between you and God.

**This month I am praying for_____.
Their specific needs are:**

Prayer Challenges

Challenge 2 - Circle Pray

This challenge is a personal favorite of mine and will complement your prayer wall. If you haven't yet delved into "The Circle Maker" by Mark Batterson, I highly recommend giving it a read. In a world accustomed to instant gratification, we often forget that prayer operates on a different timescale. While some prayers may receive prompt answers, others may unfold over years. It's essential to recognize that God's timing is distinct from our own, and His plans always prioritize our well-being.

This section serves as a dedicated space for jotting down your personal prayers. You can draw inspiration from your prayer wall, but the key aspect of this exercise is to pen your prayers as if you were directly conversing with God. A thorough execution will likely result in several pages of heartfelt communication.

Begin each day for the next 30 days by vocalizing this prayer directly to God. Over time, you will witness firsthand the tangible responses to your prayers. You are encouraged to amend and refine this prayer throughout the month as you witness God orchestrating changes in your life circumstances. This challenge holds the potential to provide remarkable insights and clarity on various aspects of your life.

Date:

My Circle Prayer

Date: **My Circle Prayer**

Date:

My Circle Prayer

> **In the beginning was the Word, & the Word was with God, & the Word was God.**
> **// John 1:1**

Let's be real friends, reading the Bible can be challenging. However, shifting focus from deciphering everything to acknowledging its living essence can be truly transformative. The Bible reflects diverse perspectives from a different era, yet its relevance remains as potent today as it was 2000 years ago.

I want to make it clear that I am not a Bible expert; I, too, encounter struggles with its content. Nonetheless, I have experienced the direct impact of God speaking to my heart at the perfect moment through this sacred text. I view the Bible as our shared past, present, and future, offering profound depth and relevance that resonates with every individual, regardless of their circumstances.

The Bible surpasses any other book in its ability to reach and touch the lives of people in every season, trial, and triumph. If you ever feel disheartened during your reading, remember this extraordinary power it holds. Your connection with God shines above merely comprehending every word and story in the Bible. Through dedication and persistence in studying, our relationship with God flourishes, alongside a deepening understanding of His living word.

> I have set my rainbow in the clouds, and it will be the sign of the covenant between me and the earth. *//Genesis 9:13*

BIBLE
Color Coding Guide

BLUE - Read through the entire passage again and underline all the names of God, Jesus, the Holy Spirit, and the Trinity in blue. Also underline the attributes of God and His character traits in blue as well.

GREEN - Read through the chapter or passage again, and this time search any commands, laws, or principles for life. Also look for references to obedience or spiritual growth and underline these mentions in green.

YELLOW - Then, read through the verses again and underline all references to eternity, heaven, or angels in yellow.

ORANGE - Use orange to underline references to sin, Satan, spiritual warfare, temptation, demons, or hell.

RED - Use red to highlight Christ, His work, prophecies regarding Christ or how He is foreshadowed in the Old Testament.

PINK - Identify relationships, love, or how to treat others and mark those in pink.

PURPLE - Use purple to mark who you are in Christ and the promises of God.

BROWN - Finally, read through the entire passage again and underline all names, times, places, locations, or numbers you come across in brown. It may be helpful to first look for proper nouns, such as 'Lazarus', and then search for times and numbers.

BLUE
Who God is, Names, Attributes

GREEN
Growth, Commands, Laws, Obedience, Fruitfulness

YELLOW
Eternity, Heaven, Angels, Hope

ORANGE
Sin, Satan, Spiritual Warfare, Temptation, Demons, or Hell

RED
Christ's atoning work, prophecy re: Christ, Christ seen in the Old Testament

PINK
Relationships, How to treat others, Love

PURPLE
Promises of God, Who I am in Christ

BROWN
Names, Times, Places, Locations, Numbers

Deep Dive Instructions

Utilize the Scripture plans to delve deeply into specific topics. Each month will feature a new theme for daily study, with enough material for one reading per day.

Every day, engage with the scripture, potentially applying the color code system for a structured review of the passage. Afterwards, reflect on the provided questions relevant to the scripture. It's acceptable not to have answers to all the questions each day, but on some days, profound insights may arise.

Bible Study
Choosing Joy

1. Psalm 16:11
2. Psalm 30:5
3. Psalm 5:11
4. Proverbs 15:13
5. Proverbs 17:22
6. Isaiah 12:3
7. Isaiah 35:10
8. Isaiah 51:11
9. Jeremiah 15:16
10. Romans 15:13
11. Galatians 5:22
12. Philippians 1:3-4
13. Philippians 4:4
14. James 1:2-3
15. James 5:13
16. 1 Peter 1:8-9
17. 1 Thess 5:16-18
18. Ecclesiastes 3:12-13
19. Zephaniah 3:17
20. Psalm 118:24
21. John 16:24
22. Philippians 3:1
23. Romans 12:12
24. Psalm 33:21
25. 2 Corinthians 7:4
26. Proverbs 10:28
27. John 15:11
28. 1 Thessalonians 1:6
29. 1 Peter 4:13
30. Psalm 126:5

Scripture_____

What is this scripture about?

What instruction, promise, wisdom or life principle did I learn from this scripture?

Scripture_____

What is this scripture about?

What instruction, promise, wisdom or life principle did I learn from this scripture?

Scripture_____

What is this scripture about?

What instruction, promise, wisdom or life principle did I learn from this scripture?

Scripture_____

What is this scripture about?

What instruction, promise, wisdom or life principle did I learn from this scripture?

Scripture_____

What is this scripture about?

What instruction, promise, wisdom or life principle did I learn from this scripture?

Scripture_____

What is this scripture about?

What instruction, promise, wisdom or life principle did I learn from this scripture?

Scripture_____

What is this scripture about?

What instruction, promise, wisdom or life principle did I learn from this scripture?

Scripture_____

What is this scripture about?

What instruction, promise, wisdom or life principle did I learn from this scripture?

Scripture_____

What is this scripture about?

What instruction, promise, wisdom or life principle did I learn from this scripture?

Scripture_____

What is this scripture about?

What instruction, promise, wisdom or life principle did I learn from this scripture?

Scripture_____

What is this scripture about?

What instruction, promise, wisdom or life principle did I learn from this scripture?

Scripture_____

What is this scripture about?

What instruction, promise, wisdom or life principle did I learn from this scripture?

Scripture_____

What is this scripture about?

What instruction, promise, wisdom or life principle did I learn from this scripture?

Scripture_____

What is this scripture about?

What instruction, promise, wisdom or life principle did I learn from this scripture?

Scripture_____

What is this scripture about?

What instruction, promise, wisdom or life principle did I learn from this scripture?

Scripture_____

What is this scripture about?

What instruction, promise, wisdom or life principle did I learn from this scripture?

Scripture_____

What is this scripture about?

What instruction, promise, wisdom or life principle did I learn from this scripture?

Scripture_____

What is this scripture about?

What instruction, promise, wisdom or life principle did I learn from this scripture?

Scripture_____

What is this scripture about?

What instruction, promise, wisdom or life principle did I learn from this scripture?

Scripture_____

What is this scripture about?

What instruction, promise, wisdom or life principle did I learn from this scripture?

Scripture_____

What is this scripture about?

What instruction, promise, wisdom or life principle did I learn from this scripture?

Scripture_____

What is this scripture about?

What instruction, promise, wisdom or life principle did I learn from this scripture?

Scripture_____

What is this scripture about?

What instruction, promise, wisdom or life principle did I learn from this scripture?

Scripture_____

What is this scripture about?

What instruction, promise, wisdom or life principle did I learn from this scripture?

Scripture_____

What is this scripture about?

What instruction, promise, wisdom or life principle did I learn from this scripture?

Scripture_____

What is this scripture about?

What instruction, promise, wisdom or life principle did I learn from this scripture?

Scripture_____

What is this scripture about?

What instruction, promise, wisdom or life principle did I learn from this scripture?

Scripture_____

What is this scripture about?

What instruction, promise, wisdom or life principle did I learn from this scripture?

Scripture_____

What is this scripture about?

What instruction, promise, wisdom or life principle did I learn from this scripture?

Scripture_____

What is this scripture about?

What instruction, promise, wisdom or life principle did I learn from this scripture?

But whoever is united with the Lord is one with him in spirit.
// 1 Corinthians 6:17

Identity Introduction

Author, trainer, and speaker Mick Mooney once shared an amazing insight that has resonated with me over the years, serving as a slice of undeniable truth. He expressed:

"One of the greatest challenges any Christian faces is the risk of falling in love with the idea of being like Jesus while failing to recognize what a life lived in his footsteps truly looks like. The life of Christ was not lived in a bubble of holy rollers, going through the same worship songs over and over, hiding away from society in their prayer meetings and revival events. Judging others from their life choices or mistakes made. Jesus was in the midst of the PARTY of life. He was at the center of the celebration, with people, all kinds of people, from all kinds of walks of life, with all kinds of world views and life styles. Jesus was in the midst of the BROKENNESS of life. When a woman was set to be stoned for her immorality, there was Jesus to defend her from the angry religious zealots. The Samaritan woman by the well, whom no one would talk with, there was Jesus starting a conversation. The lepers that no one would get close to, there was Jesus willing to touch them."

> Now you are the body of Christ, and each one of you is a part of it.
> // 1 Corinthians 12:27

Jesus didn't get a reputation amongst the religious as a 'glutton and a drunk' because of what he taught, but because he LIVED what he taught. He didn't have prostitutes crying at his feet because he preached them a sermon, but because he connected with them in a personal way, because he was not ashamed to be a genuine friend to them, and through his genuineness he was able to reveal to them that they have value, that God has not discounted them, that they are daughters of the most high God. Jesus did something we often find very difficult to do. He consistently looked for, reached out, and touched the beauty in every individual. But we can do it, surely we can, and I believe it is truly the narrow path we can walk that allows us to experience the abundant life Christ spoke of.
To look for, discover, and touch the unique and beautiful reality stored up in every individual heart. When we do this, when we truly connect with those around us in love, authenticity and grace, I believe it is then we find ourselves walking in the footsteps of our Savior." ~ Mick Mooney

It is my hope that we strive to embody the essence of Jesus as authentically as possible. While we're bound to falter at times, imagine the impact we can have on lives by giving our utmost effort.

> Jesus Christ is the same yesterday and today and forever.
> // Hebrews 13:8

What does it mean to discover your identity in Christ? Why does it matter?

It matters because it offers a solid foundation that stands unwavering. Many place their identity in temporary aspects like relationships, careers, status, and possessions, which can all be fleeting. When these are stripped away, the search begins anew, perpetuating a cycle.

Frequently, we hear of those who seem to have it all yet remain unfulfilled, sometimes resorting to harmful coping mechanisms to fill an internal void. The unchanging core identity lies solely in God and Jesus Christ. This foundation is unique in its reliability and strength. While worldly elements shift unpredictably, the Creator remains steadfast, defining our true selves.

Defining oneself through Christ provides a deep sense of purpose and belonging beyond transient worldly measures. It allows individuals to navigate life's challenges with resilience and grace, knowing they are cherished and valued unconditionally. This rootedness in faith empowers individuals to live authentically, guided by timeless principles of love, compassion, and service to others.

He predestined us for adoption to sonship through Jesus Christ, in accordance with his pleasure and will.   // Ephesians 1:5

Jesus Christ is the same yesterday and today and forever. Hebrews 13:8

How significant can an identity be if it offers deliverance from the brokenness of this world? *"Yet to all who did receive him, to those who believed in his name, he gave the right to become children of God" -John 1:12.* From the moment of our birth, we're shaped by external influences dictating our worth and capabilities. Many have endured challenging upbringings, filled with negativity and limitations that instilled feelings of inadequacy. It often takes time to realize our potential and worth, discovering our capabilities through a growing relationship with God. As we embrace our identity in Christ, we transcend worldly definitions and align with our true essence as children of God, grounding ourselves in the Creator who sees our value and potential.

Our identity diverges from the world's ideals. *"If you belonged to the world, it would love you as its own. As it is, you do not belong to the world, but I have chosen you out of the world. That is why the world hates you." - John 15:19*. This identity is profound and demands whole-hearted commitment. As children of God, it's essential to seek His guidance and strength in navigating this new role. Embracing this identity won't shield us from challenges; in fact, it may invite more struggles as we align with the Kingdom of Heaven, conflicting with the world's values. Despite potential hardships,

> but I have chosen you out of the world. That is why the world hates you
> //John 15:19

wearing the full armor of God empowers us to stand boldly. While the world may resist our faith, we cling to the promise awaiting us.

Our identity sets us apart from the world's ways, as written in John 15:19. This identity is weighty and demands our full commitment. As children of God, the next step is to seek His guidance through prayer and recognize that we cannot fulfill this role alone; it requires His strength and direction. Grounded in Christ, challenges may increase, aligning with the Kingdom of Heaven instead of worldly values. Despite potential hardships, wearing the full armor of God empowers us to stand boldly amid societal resistance, with a promise of hope in the face of trials.

Accept one another, then, just as Christ accepted you, in order to bring praise to God. // Romans 15:7

While these challenges may seem daunting, we have the assurance of a promise awaiting us. By clinging to our identity in Christ, we can navigate the trials and tribulations of life with faith and confidence. This promise sustains us through adversity and provides a beacon of hope in the midst of turmoil.

Blessed is the one who perseveres under trial because, having stood the test, that person will receive the crown of life that the Lord has promised to those who love him. James 1:12

Your new identity is the most powerful identity in the entire universe, and no matter the hardships you may face by boldly proclaiming this, know that God says this: *For we know that in all things God works for the good of those who love him, who have been called according to his purpose. (Romans 8:28)*

Identity Study

Read this scripture and answer the correlating questions.

"So do not fear, for I am with you; do not be dismayed, for I am your God. I will strengthen you and help you; I will uphold you with my righteous right hand"
Isaiah 41:10

1. What is the truth associated with this scripture?

2. What does this scripture tell me about God?

3. What does this scripture say about me?

4. What lies has the enemy been feeding me about who I am? And what Bible verse could I use to combat against this?

> But whoever is united with the Lord is one with him in spirit.
> // 1 Corinthians 6:17

Hearing Gods Voice Introduction

Get ready for a bit of an exploration as we delve into a common struggle - discerning God's voice. Throughout the past year and a half, my journey with God has centered on allowing God to guide me as a Father, leading to a closer, more conversational bond with Him. A crucial lesson emerged from this experience: God unveils deeper truths about Himself only after we've obediently followed what we already know to be right. By obeying the revealed truths, the next steps are often illuminated. This revelation has shown me the power of realizing that change is possible in our lives when we align ourselves with God's will.

Reflecting on Matthew 4:20, where individuals left everything to follow Jesus immediately, I've come to understand that following God's guidance starts with fostering a conversational relationship with Him, similar to how we interact with our loved ones. Today, consider the nature of your relationship with God and the potential for a transformative connection built on intimate conversations and obedience.

Have you cultivated a "conversational intimacy" with the Lord, or is prayer only a fleeting thought in times of need? Take a step today towards experiencing the transformative power of prayer. Embracing this practice can truly revolutionize your life.

Similar to any relationship, understanding God the Father involves a process of unveiling layers, holding meaningful conversations, and grasping His ways of communication. For those unfamiliar, the sinner's prayer serves as a point of entry into this relationship. Here is one version:

"Father, I acknowledge my wrongdoings that have distanced me from You. I am genuinely remorseful and seek to turn away from my past sins. Please forgive me, guide me away from sin, and grant me the belief in Jesus Christ, who died for my sins and rose again. I welcome Jesus as the ruler of my life, asking for the Holy Spirit's help to follow Your will. In Jesus' name, amen."

While some may view saying this prayer as an instant pathway to salvation and unity with Jesus, I see it as a door opening to your heart. It marks a significant beginning in your spiritual journey, paving the way for deeper connections and understanding with God. You're acknowledging your faults and expressing a sincere desire for change, which is a crucial initial step. However, the key aspect often overlooked is the importance of nurturing a relationship.

I, too, had recited the sinner's prayer previously but lacked a true connection with God until I cultivated an intimate relationship with Him.

Consider a marriage without quality time spent together. Imagine a couple exchanging vows and then meeting only briefly once a week through a third party, never engaging in meaningful conversations. Would they truly know each other? Similarly, knowing of someone versus knowing them intimately illustrates the distinction between mere knowledge and genuine understanding. Simply memorizing details about a person, or in the case of scripture, does not equate to a meaningful relationship.

This analogy extends to our relationship with God, emphasizing that true connection and understanding develop through intimate engagement and not just surface-level knowledge.

Growing up, I was familiar with the Bible and the teachings of Jesus, yet I lacked a personal connection with Him. Reading the Bible felt confusing and distant. However, as I began to understand God's character and how He communicates through His Son and the Holy Spirit, my perspective shifted drastically.

To truly experience this transformation, it's essential to actively engage with Jesus and to listen to God's voice speaking to us.

Understanding how God communicates with each of us is a personal journey, unique to individual experiences. However, a familiar pattern often emerges: a gentle, persistent voice followed by a subtle nudge, which gradually becomes clearer with undeniable confirmation. This communication may manifest in various forms - repetitive number sequences, whispered words, timely songs with poignant lyrics, unexpected phone calls from friends, or even messages seemingly tailored for you on billboards, social media, or through daily reflections like a Bible verse or devotion.

While some may perceive these occurrences as mere coincidence, chance, serendipity, happenstance or fate, I urge you to consider that God is the ultimate Author and Creator, encompassing the past, present, and future. Chance, serendipity, happenstance and fate do not confirm their appearance, the definition of chance is: the occurrence and development of events in the absence of any obvious design. When God is speaking there is and obvious design. And he will confirm it to you, that is how you will know the difference.

Personally, I do not believe in coincidences, chance, or serendipity, but rather in fate as part of a grander design orchestrated by God. As you embark on a journey to know Jesus and spend time with Him, you will gradually recognize the ways in which God communicates with you. This process will lead to personal growth and a deeper understanding of Him, unveiling a remarkable love story between your heart and the Creator.

However, I must caution you that falling in love with your Heavenly Father will bring about profound changes in your life. Your heart will soften, and moments of indescribable joy may unexpectedly fill your days. You might find yourself moved to tears contemplating the immense sacrifice of Jesus on the cross, evoking emotions unlike any you've ever experienced.

Numerous individuals from diverse religious backgrounds, including Muslims and Hindus, have shared accounts of encountering Christ. One common thread among these experiences is the unparalleled presence of the Holy Spirit. The uniqueness and beauty of the Holy Spirit's influence cannot be paralleled by any other force, offering a transformative and awe-inspiring connection to God.

Revelation 3:20 -
Behold, I stand at the door, and knock: if any man hear my voice, and open the door, I will come in to him, and will sup with him, and he with me.

Jeremiah 33:3
Call to me and I will answer you, and will tell you great and hidden things that you have not known.

    A crucial aspect that is frequently overlooked, both in ancient times when Jesus roamed the earth over 2000 years ago and in present-day, is the resemblance of the Pharisees' mentality. Often, individuals become fixated on legalistic interpretations and doctrines, losing sight of the core message that Jesus advocated during his ministry: love, acceptance, tolerance, faith, and belief. People can become entangled in rigid interpretations of Bible verses and adherence to laws, sidelining the essence of building a genuine relationship with God.

Matthew 23:1-8
Then Jesus said to the crowds and to his disciples, "The teachers of religious law and the Pharisees are the official interpreters of the law of Moses. So practice and obey whatever they tell you, but don't follow their example. For they don't practice what they teach. They crush people with unbearable religious demands and never lift a finger to ease the burden.
"Everything they do is for show. On their arms they wear extra wide prayer boxes with Scripture verses inside, and they wear robes with extra long tassels.

And they love to sit at the head table at banquets and in the seats of honor in the synagogues. They love to receive respectful greetings as they walk in the marketplaces, and to be called 'Rabbi.' "Don't let anyone call you 'Rabbi,' for you have only one teacher, and all of you are equal as brothers and sisters. And don't address anyone here on earth as 'Father,' for only God in heaven is your Father. And don't let anyone call you 'Teacher,' for you have only one teacher, the Messiah. The greatest among you must be a servant. But those who exalt themselves will be humbled, and those who humble themselves will be exalted.

Luke 18:10-14 ESV
"Two men went up into the temple to pray, one a Pharisee and the other a tax collector. The Pharisee, standing by himself, prayed thus: 'God, I thank you that I am not like other men, extortions, unjust, adulterers, or even like this tax collector. I fast twice a week; I give tithes of all that I get.' But the tax collector, standing far off, would not even lift up his eyes to heaven, but beat his breast, saying, 'God, be merciful to me, a sinner!' I tell you, this man went down to his house justified, rather than the other. For everyone who exalts himself will be humbled, but the one who humbles himself will be exalted."

The Pharisees appeared to fulfill all the right outward actions and held significant power, yet they often displayed disdain towards those considered less important. Contrarily, Jesus chose to surround himself with the overlooked and marginalized individuals, recognizing that genuine righteousness stemmed from matters of the heart, rather than mere external appearances.

The Pharisees prayed to avoid resembling the poor and the less privileged, revealing a lack of humility before God. Throughout my years of interactions, I have encountered individuals who struggle with reading the Bible and long to experience God's presence. They often feel inadequate in interpreting the text as they believe they should. My guidance to them is this: Focus on nurturing your relationship with God, cultivate the ability to listen and connect with Him, and His word will begin to resonate with you deeply.

Consider the criminal who hung on the cross beside Jesus during His crucifixion. Did he possess knowledge of the Bible or strictly adhere to its laws? It seems unlikely. Yet, when reflecting on the interaction between the criminal and Jesus, it is apparent that faith and relationship with Christ transcended any need for Biblical knowledge or strict adherence to laws.

Luke 23: 32-43
Two others, both criminals, were led out to be executed with him. When they came to a place called The Skull they nailed him to the cross. And the criminals were also crucified—one on his right and one on his left.
Jesus said, "Father, forgive them, for they don't know what they are doing." And the soldiers gambled for his clothes by throwing dice.
The crowd watched and the leaders scoffed. "He saved others," they said, "let him save himself if he is really God's Messiah, the Chosen One." The soldiers mocked him, too, by offering him a drink of sour wine. They called out to him, "If you are the King of the Jews, save yourself!" A sign was fastened above him with these words: "This is the King of the Jews."

One of the criminals hanging beside him scoffed, "So you're the Messiah, are you? Prove it by saving yourself—and us, too, while you're at it!" But the other criminal protested, "Don't you fear God even when you have been sentenced to die? We deserve to die for our crimes, but this man hasn't done anything wrong." Then he said, "Jesus, remember me when you come into your Kingdom." And Jesus replied, "I assure you, today you will be with me in paradise."

As he neared the end of his life, the criminal beside Jesus epitomized true humility by acknowledging his mistakes, seeking forgiveness, and expressing faith. It was his sincere repentance and request for forgiveness that mattered most, not the ability to recite scripture from memory. God's intention was never for the relationship with Him to be arduous or perplexing. The Bible serves as a guide, bridging ancient history with the inception of salvation history, offering insight into the past, present, and future. However, the essence of the matter lies in fostering a deep relationship with God, for He assesses the sincerity of one's heart. Our duty is not to judge, but to understand that genuine connection with God surpasses mere good deeds. It is essential to prioritize knowing God intimately over merely studying and comprehending every chapter of the Bible.

While maintaining reverence for the Word, it is crucial to shift focus towards nurturing a personal relationship with God. Understand that the Bible can serve as a valuable instrument for receiving confirmations and insights from the Lord.

Over the next few pages I am excited to share some amazing testimonies from my fellow Brothers and Sisters in Christ, who have graciously allowed me to impart their stories to you. By delving into these narratives, I trust that you will begin to discern how God communicates and recognize similarities with your own experiences. These accounts are intended to awaken within you a heightened sense of awareness, enabling you to recognize His voice more readily in your daily life. Remember, God's voice can come through in various ways and through individuals. Keeping this in mind, let us take a collective journey through the following stories, and be inspired by the remarkable ways in which God speaks and confirms His presence.

Behold I come Quickly!

    A fellow Brother in Christ named Todd experienced a significant awakening in 2011. Here is his testimonial:
Towards the end of 2010 and into the early months of 2011, Todd started encountering the number 311 in various unexpected places - on billboards, license plates, while tidying up closets and stumbling upon old 311 album, and even on the clock. The omnipresence of this number began to haunt him, prompting him to mention it to his family. Feeling a deep conviction that it held a greater significance, Todd initiated prayers, seeking clarity on its meaning.

During a family vacation in Florida in early March, Todd found himself unable to shake off the persistent feeling connected to this number. On the 10th of that month, after retiring to bed, he experienced an exceptionally vivid dream that deeply impacted him. This dream left an indelible impression, the kind that lingers for days on end. Upon awakening, Todd recounted the dream to his family, detailing how he had dreamt of a catastrophic earthquake in Japan resulting in mass casualties. Initially met with skepticism by his family, dismissing it as a mere byproduct of a late-night meal, their perception swiftly shifted. As they made their way to breakfast, they were met with a crowd transfixed by a television screen broadcasting breaking news - a devastating earthquake had indeed struck Japan, triggering a catastrophic tsunami that caused widespread destruction. Witnessing this unfolding tragedy, Todd's premonition manifested as a chilling reality, leaving him and his family astounded by the accuracy of his prophetic dream.

After the profound events that transpired, Todd found himself in deep contemplation, earnestly seeking divine guidance through prayer. Wrestling with the purpose behind being granted such foresight, Todd was overwhelmed with emotion upon realizing the significance of the date—March 11th, represented by the numbers 3-11. Overcome with emotion, he knelt in tears, grappling with the mystery of this revelation.

In the following weeks, Todd undertook diligent research in pursuit of answers. During his quest for clarity, a quiet yet compelling inner voice directed him to delve into his Bible, particularly the book of Revelation. Turning to *Revelation 3:11, he read the verse: "Behold, I come quickly: hold that fast which thou hast, that no man take thy crown."*

This scripture stirred his spirit, prompting Todd to wonder whether it served as a subtle warning, urging vigilance as the return of Jesus drew near. Encountering this message ignited a spiritual reawakening within him. Subsequently, Todd began a journey, establishing a Youtube Ministry that touched the lives of countless individuals, leading them to a relationship with Christ.

While refraining from delving deeply into apocalyptic prophecies, Todd's experience serves as a poignant reminder of the spiritual significance pervading our world today. Encouraging a deeper connection with God, Todd's narrative, alongside others like his own, highlights the personal ways in which God communicates with each of us, inviting us into a sacred dialogue filled with love and hope.

White Doves

This remarkable account is shared by my dear Brother in Christ, Jamie, whose narrative embodies a true miracle—a testament to the wonder of God's grace.

In the tumultuous year of 2008, amid the economic downturn that shook the very foundation of society, Jamie, the proprietor of Stamm Heating and Cooling in Waynesville, Ohio, found his business significantly impacted by the financial crisis. Like many small business owners, he felt the stark repercussions of the economic turbulence, witnessing a divide between the privileged and the struggling as prosperity seemed to slip further from his grasp. Amidst the shadows of uncertainty and adversity, Jamie grappled with questions, questioning why God seemingly remained distant in his time of need, causing him to doubt the loving care he once believed in.

An evening marked by weariness and desperation found Jamie seeking solace in prayer, yearning for a glimmer of divine reassurance. Sitting in his idling car in the driveway, Jamie poured out his heart in prayer, pleading for a sign from God—an unmistakable symbol of His presence and providence. He asked God " If you are there, please send me a sign. Send me a Dove as a messenger so I know you hear me." Yet, as moments turned into minutes, the anticipated dove failed to materialize, leaving Jamie disheartened and embittered by the perceived silence of God.

Disheartened and disillusioned, Jamie's faith faltered as he resigned himself to disappointment, muttering his discontent towards the heavens. However, in that moment of despair, a miraculous turn of events unfolded, ushering in a divine intervention and offering Jamie a glimmer of hope amidst his turmoil.

Making his way towards his house, Jamie was struck by a breathtaking sight: a multitude of doves perched along the gutters encircling his home, with more nestled in the pine tree nearby. Overwhelmed by the unprecedented gathering of these symbolic birds, Jamie stood in astonishment, silently contemplating the divine display before him.

In a moment of revelation, Jamie heard a gentle whisper within his soul. God's voice, tender and reassuring, resonated within him, declaring, "My son, I love you not as one dove, but as many." This message, delivered in a soft, still tone, stirred Jamie to the core, evoking a sense of awe and wonder at the boundless love bestowed upon him. The powerful realization of God's all-encompassing love left Jamie in awe, a testament of divine intervention and grace that never fails to amaze.

Isaiah 41:13
For I, the Lord your God, hold your right hand; it is I who say to you, "Fear not, I am the one who helps you."

Love is Patient

　I'm sure many of you can relate to this scenario, but just wait until you see how God steps in at the end. It was a typical Sunday morning, and we were predictably behind schedule for church, tensions running high within our family. Sound familiar? It's what we call spiritual warfare, with the enemy working hard to disrupt our peace and unity. As we hurriedly corralled the kids into the car, it was evident that Matt, my husband, was on edge, his patience wearing thin, particularly towards me, marked by a few cutting remarks.

The tipping point came when Matt muttered under his breath about the state of the bath towels. I tried to explain, "I'm so sorry about the laundry not being done; I've been swamped studying for my Real Estate Exam." But he seemed more frustrated about not finding a clean towel than the laundry itself. Apparently, his missing towel after his shower was the final straw. He expressed his exasperation, "It's not just about today. It's about our entire history of me not having my towel when I need it, despite hanging it up for that exact reason." A revelation to me, to say the least.

While seething inwardly, I chose to stay silent, taking deep breaths and resisting the urge to list all the times he's had his own quirks and flaws throughout our relationship. The car ride was filled with tension, but I wrestled with my emotions, refraining from unloading past grievances during that moment.

I decided to entrust the situation to God because I knew that speaking my mind at that moment would only escalate things further.

During the church service, the pastor spoke about spiritual warfare and the importance of approaching every situation with love. It was as if he had been eavesdropping on our car conversation between Matt and me, using it as a real-life example for his sermon. He highlighted a familiar scripture, *1 Corinthians 13: 4-5*, which talks about the nature of love - being patient, kind, not keeping record of wrongs, and more.

The mention of not keeping a record of wrongs struck a chord with me, especially considering the ongoing towel saga in our relationship. It was even more poignant because the same scripture had been read at our wedding. It felt like a gentle nudge from God to remind Matt of our vows and the essence of unconditional love. I mentioned this to Matt afterwards, and he chuckled and apologized. It was a simple yet impactful moment of correction facilitated by God. It made me reflect on the importance of being attuned to God's messages in our everyday mundane lives.

In Conclusion

    I have many stories like this; maybe one day I'll gather them into a book. But for now, this is a good beginning. As we proceed with some exercises, keep in mind a simple method I've found helpful in distinguishing my thoughts from those I believe are from God - it's when sudden ideas or thoughts appear out of nowhere. Sometimes, I'll be thinking about lunch options and then a grand scheme to combat climate change drops into my mind. It's a rather extreme example, and my thoughts on climate change are a different topic altogether. But you get the gist. When unfamiliar thoughts or words intrude my mind, prompting me to research them, that's when I sense God communicating. It's usually beyond my usual scope and comfort zone.

Now, let's delve into some questions on discerning God's voice from our own. Take note of the checklist provided below. It's a good practice to seek three confirmations. Documenting how these confirmations manifest can enhance your ability to discern quickly and with confidence in the future.

Lastly, remember that God understands your inner being and knows the most effective way to communicate with you. Personally, I notice patterns in numbers, specific ones that have appeared throughout my life. Have you experienced this as well? That's one way God may communicate with you. By understanding these signs, we can establish a clear channel to hear God's voice unmistakably.

Discerning God's Voice

Date-

Word or thought that passed through my head?

Is there a scripture that reflects this?

What does this thought mean to me, if anything?

Will it bring forth the Kingdom of God?

Will this bring forth good fruit?

Confirmation Checklist

☐ How?   ☐ How?   ☐ How?

Discerning God's Voice

Date-

___

Word or thought that passed through my head?

Is there a scripture that reflects this?

What does this thought mean to me, if anything?

Will it bring forth the Kingdom of God?

Will this bring forth good fruit?

___

Confirmation Checklist

☐ How? ☐ How? ☐ How?

Discerning God's Voice

Date- _____

Word or thought that passed through my head?

Is there a scripture that reflects this?

What does this thought mean to me, if anything?

Will it bring forth the Kingdom of God?

Will this bring forth good fruit?

Confirmation Checklist

☐ How?   ☐ How?   ☐ How?

Obedience

What is God asking me to do?

Does this take me outside of my comfort zone?

Does it have the potential to be life changing for me or for someone else?

What would happen if I didn't do it?

What would happen if I did?

Final Outcome

Obedience

What is God asking me to do?

Does this take me outside of my comfort zone?

Does it have the potential to be life changing for me or for someone else?

What would happen if I didn't do it?

What would happen if I did?

Final Outcome

> For thus has LORD said to me, Go, set a watchman. Let him declare what he sees. //Isaiah 21:6

Watchman Introduction

When I was called back to the Lord in 2011 God opened the flood gates to me about prophesy. There were many that he called at this time. He called me to be a watchman/woman on the wall for the second coming of Jesus. I lost friends, put strain on my marriage and most people thought I had lost my mind, and for a few years, maybe I had, but it was all for the Lord. Let's not forget how many people laughed at Noah as he built a ridiculously large boat.

What I didn't understand at that time is that not everyone is called to this position. And that is ok! But if you have a burning desire to read and understand Revelation and a unexplained urgency in your spirit to warn and share how Bible prophecy is being fulfilled then you might just have been called to me a watchmen.

One last thing, I do not know when Jesus is returning. The Bible says no man will know the day or hour. However he does command us to know and discern the times. To be watchful and prepared. Use this section to keep track of world events and how they fit into the end time puzzle. Use the resources that I have cultivated over the last 10 years that have taught me and also calmed my nerves when things start to get a little bumpy.
And finally, if God has called you to this position, he will make a way for you!

Prophecy Notes

Date:

Today's Note Worthy Events:

Correlating Scripture:

What do I think this means?

Prophecy Notes

Date:

Today's Note Worthy Events:

Correlating Scripture:

What do I think this means?

Prophecy Notes

Date:

Today's Note Worthy Events:

Correlating Scripture:

What do I think this means?

Resources

https://www.jdfarag.org/bible-prophecyvents

https://www.youtube.com/c/firecharger/featured

https://www.youtube.com/watch?v=I55So_jR5lk
This is the trailer of a movie I highly reccommend

Rooted

month
―――――――――――

Important Events

MONTH **YEAR**

Sunday	Monday	Tuesday	Wednesday	Thursday	Friday	Saturday

MY NOTES

MY NOTES

MY NOTES

My Prayer Wall
"Prayer is Adventurous"

For Others:

[Y] Answered [N]

How has God answered or shifted this prayer?

For Myself:

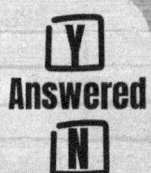

[Y] Answered [N]

How has God answered or shifted this prayer?

My Prayer Wall
"Prayer is Adventurous"

For Others:

[Y] Answered [N]

How has God answered or shifted this prayer?

For Myself:

[Y] Answered [N]

How has God answered or shifted this prayer?

My Prayer Wall
"Prayer is Adventurous"

For Others:

[Y] Answered [N]

How has God answered or shifted this prayer?

For Myself:

[Y] Answered [N]

How has God answered or shifted this prayer?

Prayer Challenges

Challenge 1 - Secret Prayer

This month I am praying for _____
Their specific needs are:

Date:

My Circle Prayer

Date: **My Circle Prayer**

Date:

My Circle Prayer

> I have set my rainbow in the clouds, and it will be the sign of the covenant between me and the earth. //Genesis 9:13

BIBLE
Color Coding Guide

BLUE - Read through the entire passage again and underline all the names of God, Jesus, the Holy Spirit, and the Trinity in blue. Also underline the attributes of God and His character traits in blue as well.

GREEN - Read through the chapter or passage again, and this time search any commands, laws, or principles for life. Also look for references to obedience or spiritual growth and underline these mentions in green.

YELLOW - Then, read through the verses again and underline all references to eternity, heaven, or angels in yellow.

ORANGE - Use orange to underline references to sin, Satan, spiritual warfare, temptation, demons, or hell.

RED - Use red to highlight Christ, His work, prophecies regarding Christ or how He is foreshadowed in the Old Testament.

PINK - Identify relationships, love, or how to treat others and mark those in pink.

PURPLE - Use purple to mark who you are in Christ and the promises of God.

BROWN - Finally, read through the entire passage again and underline all names, times, places, locations, or numbers you come across in brown. It may be helpful to first look for proper nouns, such as 'Lazarus', and then search for times and numbers.

BLUE — Who God is, Names, Attributes

GREEN — Growth, Commands, Laws, Obedience, Fruitfulness

YELLOW — Eternity, Heaven, Angels, Hope

ORANGE — Sin, Satan, Spiritual Warfare, Temptation, Demons, or Hell

RED — Christ's atoning work, prophecy re: Christ, Christ seen in the Old Testament

PINK — Relationships, How to treat others, Love

PURPLE — Promises of God, Who I am in Christ

BROWN — Names, Times, Places, Locations, Numbers

Bible Study
Money Matters

1. Proverbs 23:4-5
2. I John 2:15-17.
3. Philippians 4:11-13
4. Matthew 6:24
5. II Corinthians 9:7
6. Proverbs 15:27
7. Mark 8:36
8. Proverbs 22:7
9. Matthew 5:42
10. Mark 4:19
11. Proverbs 13:11
12. Proverbs 3:27
13. Proverbs 14:23
14. Proverbs 11:4
15. Luke 14:28-30
16. Proverbs 13:22
17. Matthew 6:24
18. James 5"1-6
19. Proverbs 22:1
20. 1 Corinthians 16:2
21. Proverbs 12:9
22. 1 Timothy 6:6-12
23. Proverbs 28:25
24. Proverbs 10:4
25. Matthew 6:2-5
26. Matthew 25:14-30
27. Proverbs 22:26-27
28. Ecclesiastes 5:10
29. 1 Timothy 6:17-19
30. Matthew 19:21-24

Scripture_____

What is this scripture about?

What instruction, promise, wisdom or life principle did I learn from this scripture?

Scripture_____

What is this scripture about?

What instruction, promise, wisdom or life principle did I learn from this scripture?

Scripture_____

What is this scripture about?

What instruction, promise, wisdom or life principle did I learn from this scripture?

Scripture_____

What is this scripture about?

What instruction, promise, wisdom or life principle did I learn from this scripture?

Scripture_____

What is this scripture about?

What instruction, promise, wisdom or life principle did I learn from this scripture?

Scripture_____

What is this scripture about?

What instruction, promise, wisdom or life principle did I learn from this scripture?

Scripture_____

What is this scripture about?

What instruction, promise, wisdom or life principle did I learn from this scripture?

Scripture_____

What is this scripture about?

What instruction, promise, wisdom or life principle did I learn from this scripture?

Scripture_____

What is this scripture about?

What instruction, promise, wisdom or life principle did I learn from this scripture?

Scripture_____

What is this scripture about?

What instruction, promise, wisdom or life principle did I learn from this scripture?

Scripture_____

What is this scripture about?

What instruction, promise, wisdom or life principle did I learn from this scripture?

Scripture_____

What is this scripture about?

What instruction, promise, wisdom or life principle did I learn from this scripture?

Scripture_____

What is this scripture about?

What instruction, promise, wisdom or life principle did I learn from this scripture?

Scripture_____

What is this scripture about?

What instruction, promise, wisdom or life principle did I learn from this scripture?

Scripture_____

What is this scripture about?

What instruction, promise, wisdom or life principle did I learn from this scripture?

Scripture_____

What is this scripture about?

What instruction, promise, wisdom or life principle did I learn from this scripture?

Scripture_____

What is this scripture about?

What instruction, promise, wisdom or life principle did I learn from this scripture?

Scripture_____

What is this scripture about?

What instruction, promise, wisdom or life principle did I learn from this scripture?

Scripture_____

What is this scripture about?

What instruction, promise, wisdom or life principle did I learn from this scripture?

Scripture_____

What is this scripture about?

What instruction, promise, wisdom or life principle did I learn from this scripture?

Scripture_____

What is this scripture about?

What instruction, promise, wisdom or life principle did I learn from this scripture?

Scripture_____

What is this scripture about?

What instruction, promise, wisdom or life principle did I learn from this scripture?

Scripture_____

What is this scripture about?

What instruction, promise, wisdom or life principle did I learn from this scripture?

Scripture_____

What is this scripture about?

What instruction, promise, wisdom or life principle did I learn from this scripture?

Scripture_____

What is this scripture about?

What instruction, promise, wisdom or life principle did I learn from this scripture?

Scripture_____

What is this scripture about?

What instruction, promise, wisdom or life principle did I learn from this scripture?

Scripture_____

What is this scripture about?

What instruction, promise, wisdom or life principle did I learn from this scripture?

Scripture_____

What is this scripture about?

What instruction, promise, wisdom or life principle did I learn from this scripture?

Scripture_____

What is this scripture about?

What instruction, promise, wisdom or life principle did I learn from this scripture?

Scripture_____

What is this scripture about?

What instruction, promise, wisdom or life principle did I learn from this scripture?

Identity Study

Read this scripture and answer the correlating questions.

Trust in the Lord with all your heart and lean not on your own understanding in all your ways submit to him, and he will make your paths straight.
Proverbs 3: 5-6

1. What is the truth associated with this scripture?

2. What does this scripture tell me about God?

3. What does this scripture say about me?

4. What lies has the enemy been feeding me about who I am? And what Bible verse could I use to combat against this?

Discerning God's Voice

Date-

Word or thought that passed through my head?

Is there a scripture that reflects this?

What does this thought mean to me, if anything?

Will it bring forth the Kingdom of God?

Will this bring forth good fruit?

Confirmation Checklist

☐ How?   ☐ How?   ☐ How?

Discerning God's Voice

Date-

Word or thought that passed through my head?

Is there a scripture that reflects this?

What does this thought mean to me, if anything?

Will it bring forth the Kingdom of God?

Will this bring forth good fruit?

Confirmation Checklist

☐ How? ☐ How? ☐ How?

Discerning God's Voice

Date- _____

Word or thought that passed through my head?

Is there a scripture that reflects this?

What does this thought mean to me, if anything?

Will it bring forth the Kingdom of God?

Will this bring forth good fruit?

_____

Confirmation Checklist

☐ How?   ☐ How?   ☐ How?

Obedience

What is God asking me to do?

Does this take me outside of my comfort zone?

Does it have the potential to be life changing for me or for someone else?

What would happen if I didn't do it?

What would happen if I did?

Final Outcome

Obedience

What is God asking me to do?

Does this take me outside of my comfort zone?

Does it have the potential to be life changing for me or for someone else?

What would happen if I didn't do it?

What would happen if I did?

Final Outcome

Prophecy Notes

Date:

Today's Note Worthy Events:

Correlating Scripture:

What do I think this means?

Prophecy Notes

Date:

Today's Note Worthy Events:

Correlating Scripture:

What do I think this means?

Prophecy Notes

Date:

Today's Note Worthy Events:

Correlating Scripture:

What do I think this means?

Rooted

month

_____

Important Events

MONTH   **YEAR**

Sunday	Monday	Tuesday	Wednesday	Thursday	Friday	Saturday

MY NOTES

MY NOTES

MY NOTES

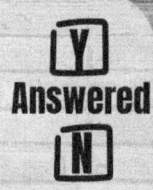

My Prayer Wall
"Prayer is Adventurous"

For Others:

[Y] Answered [N]

How has God answered or shifted this prayer?

For Myself:

[Y] Answered [N]

How has God answered or shifted this prayer?

My Prayer Wall
"Prayer is Adventurous"

For Others:

[Y] Answered [N]

How has God answered or shifted this prayer?

For Myself:

[Y] Answered [N]

How has God answered or shifted this prayer?

My Prayer Wall
"Prayer is Adventurous"

For Others:

Answered: [Y] [N]

How has God answered or shifted this prayer?

For Myself:

Answered: [Y] [N]

How has God answered or shifted this prayer?

Prayer Challenges

Challenge 1 - Secret Prayer

This month I am praying for_____
Their specific needs are:

Date:

My Circle Prayer

Date:

My Circle Prayer

Date:

My Circle Prayer

> I have set my rainbow in the clouds, and it will be the sign of the covenant between me and the earth.   //Genesis 9:13

BIBLE
Color Coding Guide

BLUE - Read through the entire passage again and underline all the names of God, Jesus, the Holy Spirit, and the Trinity in blue. Also underline the attributes of God and His character traits in blue as well.

GREEN - Read through the chapter or passage again, and this time search any commands, laws, or principles for life. Also look for references to obedience or spiritual growth and underline these mentions in green.

YELLOW - Then, read through the verses again and underline all references to eternity, heaven, or angels in yellow.

ORANGE - Use orange to underline references to sin, Satan, spiritual warfare, temptation, demons, or hell.

RED - Use red to highlight Christ, His work, prophecies regarding Christ or how He is foreshadowed in the Old Testament.

PINK - Identify relationships, love, or how to treat others and mark those in pink.

PURPLE - Use purple to mark who you are in Christ and the promises of God.

BROWN - Finally, read through the entire passage again and underline all names, times, places, locations, or numbers you come across in brown. It may be helpful to first look for proper nouns, such as 'Lazarus', and then search for times and numbers.

BLUE — Who God is, Names, Attributes

GREEN — Growth, Commands, Laws, Obedience, Fruitfulness

YELLOW — Eternity, Heaven, Angels, Hope

ORANGE — Sin, Satan, Spiritual Warfare, Temptation, Demons, or Hell

RED — Christ's atoning work, prophecy re: Christ, Christ seen in the Old Testament

PINK — Relationships, How to treat others, Love

PURPLE — Promises of God, Who I am in Christ

BROWN — Names, Times, Places, Locations, Numbers

Bible Study
Living in Gratitude

1. Psalm 75:1
2. Luke 22:19
3. Colossians 4:1-6
4. Revelation 7:12
5. 1 Thessalonians 5:18
6. Psalm 107:1
7. 2 Corinthians 4:14-15
8. Philemon 1:4
9. Psalm 100:1-5
10. John 14:1
11. Psalm 14:1
12. Ephesians 2:8
13. Colossians 2:7
14. Lamentations 3:23-24
15. 1 chronicles 29:13
16. Philippians 4:6
17. Isaiah 12:4
18. Psalm 28:7
19. Hebrews 12:28
20. Jeremiah 33:11
21. Psalm 69:30
22. 1 Corinthians 1:4
23. Colossians 3:16
24. John 3:16
25. Psalm 27:14
26. Jonah 2:9
27. Daniel 2:23
28. James 1:17
29. Isaiah 43:1-2
30. Psalm 9:1

Scripture_____

What is this scripture about?

What instruction, promise, wisdom or life principle did I learn from this scripture?

Scripture_____

What is this scripture about?

What instruction, promise, wisdom or life principle did I learn from this scripture?

Scripture_____

What is this scripture about?

What instruction, promise, wisdom or life principle did I learn from this scripture?

Scripture_____

What is this scripture about?

What instruction, promise, wisdom or life principle did I learn from this scripture?

Scripture_____

What is this scripture about?

What instruction, promise, wisdom or life principle did I learn from this scripture?

Scripture_____

What is this scripture about?

What instruction, promise, wisdom or life principle did I learn from this scripture?

Scripture_____

What is this scripture about?

What instruction, promise, wisdom or life principle did I learn from this scripture?

Scripture_____

What is this scripture about?

What instruction, promise, wisdom or life principle did I learn from this scripture?

Scripture_____

What is this scripture about?

What instruction, promise, wisdom or life principle did I learn from this scripture?

Scripture_____

What is this scripture about?

What instruction, promise, wisdom or life principle did I learn from this scripture?

Scripture_____

What is this scripture about?

What instruction, promise, wisdom or life principle did I learn from this scripture?

Scripture_____

What is this scripture about?

What instruction, promise, wisdom or life principle did I learn from this scripture?

Scripture_____

What is this scripture about?

What instruction, promise, wisdom or life principle did I learn from this scripture?

Scripture_____

What is this scripture about?

What instruction, promise, wisdom or life principle did I learn from this scripture?

Scripture_____

What is this scripture about?

What instruction, promise, wisdom or life principle did I learn from this scripture?

Scripture_____

What is this scripture about?

What instruction, promise, wisdom or life principle did I learn from this scripture?

Scripture_____

What is this scripture about?

What instruction, promise, wisdom or life principle did I learn from this scripture?

Scripture_____

What is this scripture about?

What instruction, promise, wisdom or life principle did I learn from this scripture?

Scripture_____

What is this scripture about?

What instruction, promise, wisdom or life principle did I learn from this scripture?

Scripture_____

What is this scripture about?

What instruction, promise, wisdom or life principle did I learn from this scripture?

Scripture_____

What is this scripture about?

What instruction, promise, wisdom or life principle did I learn from this scripture?

Scripture_____

What is this scripture about?

What instruction, promise, wisdom or life principle did I learn from this scripture?

Scripture_____

What is this scripture about?

What instruction, promise, wisdom or life principle did I learn from this scripture?

Scripture_____

What is this scripture about?

What instruction, promise, wisdom or life principle did I learn from this scripture?

Scripture_____

What is this scripture about?

What instruction, promise, wisdom or life principle did I learn from this scripture?

Scripture_____

What is this scripture about?

What instruction, promise, wisdom or life principle did I learn from this scripture?

Scripture_____

What is this scripture about?

What instruction, promise, wisdom or life principle did I learn from this scripture?

Scripture_____

What is this scripture about?

What instruction, promise, wisdom or life principle did I learn from this scripture?

Scripture_____

What is this scripture about?

What instruction, promise, wisdom or life principle did I learn from this scripture?

Scripture_____

What is this scripture about?

What instruction, promise, wisdom or life principle did I learn from this scripture?

Identity Study

Read this scripture and answer the correlating questions.

Therefore, if anyone is in Christ, the new creation has come:[a] The old has gone, the new is here! All this is from God, who reconciled us to himself through Christ and gave us the ministry of reconciliation: that God was reconciling the world to himself in Christ, not counting people's sins against them. And he has committed to us the message of reconciliation.
2 Corinthians 5: 17-19

1. What is the truth associated with this scripture?

2. What does this scripture tell me about God?

3. What does this scripture say about me?

4. What lies has the enemy been feeding me about who I am? And what Bible verse could I use to combat against this?

Discerning God's Voice

Date- _____

Word or thought that passed through my head?

Is there a scripture that reflects this?

What does this thought mean to me, if anything?

Will it bring forth the Kingdom of God?

Will this bring forth good fruit?

Confirmation Checklist

☐ How?   ☐ How?   ☐ How?

Discerning God's Voice

Date-

Word or thought that passed through my head?

Is there a scripture that reflects this?

What does this thought mean to me, if anything?

Will it bring forth the Kingdom of God?

Will this bring forth good fruit?

Confirmation Checklist

☐ How?   ☐ How?   ☐ How?

Discerning God's Voice

Date- _____

Word or thought that passed through my head?

Is there a scripture that reflects this?

What does this thought mean to me, if anything?

Will it bring forth the Kingdom of God?

Will this bring forth good fruit?

_____

Confirmation Checklist

☐ How? ☐ How? ☐ How?

Obedience

What is God asking me to do?

Does this take me outside of my comfort zone?

Does it have the potential to be life changing for me or for someone else?

What would happen if I didn't do it?

What would happen if I did?

Final Outcome

Obedience

What is God asking me to do?

Does this take me outside of my comfort zone?

Does it have the potential to be life changing for me or for someone else?

What would happen if I didn't do it?

What would happen if I did?

Final Outcome

Prophecy Notes

Date:

Today's Note Worthy Events:

Correlating Scripture:

What do I think this means?

Prophecy Notes

Date:

Today's Note Worthy Events:

Correlating Scripture:

What do I think this means?

Prophecy Notes

Date:

Today's Note Worthy Events:

Correlating Scripture:

What do I think this means?

Rooted

month
_____

Important Events

MONTH   **YEAR**

Sunday	Monday	Tuesday	Wednesday	Thursday	Friday	Saturday

MY NOTES

MY NOTES

MY NOTES

My Prayer Wall
"Prayer is Adventurous"

For Others:

Y
Answered
N

How has God answered or shifted this prayer?

For Myself:

Y
Answered
N

How has God answered or shifted this prayer?

My Prayer Wall
"Prayer is Adventurous"

For Others:

[Y] Answered
[N]

How has God answered or shifted this prayer?

For Myself:

[Y] Answered
[N]

How has God answered or shifted this prayer?

My Prayer Wall
"Prayer is Adventurous"

For Others:

Answered: Y / N

How has God answered or shifted this prayer?

For Myself:

Answered: Y / N

How has God answered or shifted this prayer?

Prayer Challenges

Challenge 1 - Secret Prayer

This month I am praying for_____
Their specific needs are:

Date:

My Circle Prayer

Date:

My Circle Prayer

Date:

My Circle Prayer

> I have set my rainbow in the clouds, and it will be the sign of the covenant between me and the earth. //Genesis 9:13

BLUE - Read through the entire passage again and underline all the names of God, Jesus, the Holy Spirit, and the Trinity in blue. Also underline the attributes of God and His character traits in blue as well.

GREEN - Read through the chapter or passage again, and this time search any commands, laws, or principles for life. Also look for references to obedience or spiritual growth and underline these mentions in green.

YELLOW - Then, read through the verses again and underline all references to eternity, heaven, or angels in yellow.

ORANGE - Use orange to underline references to sin, Satan, spiritual warfare, temptation, demons, or hell.

RED - Use red to highlight Christ, His work, prophecies regarding Christ or how He is foreshadowed in the Old Testament.

PINK - Identify relationships, love, or how to treat others and mark those in pink.

PURPLE - Use purple to mark who you are in Christ and the promises of God.

BROWN - Finally, read through the entire passage again and underline all names, times, places, locations, or numbers you come across in brown. It may be helpful to first look for proper nouns, such as 'Lazarus', and then search for times and numbers.

BIBLE
Color Coding Guide

BLUE
Who God is, Names, Attributes

GREEN
Growth, Commands, Laws, Obedience, Fruitfulness

YELLOW
Eternity, Heaven, Angels, Hope

ORANGE
Sin, Satan, Spiritual Warfare, Temptation, Demons, or Hell

RED
Christ's atoning work, prophecy re: Christ, Christ seen in the Old Testament

PINK
Relationships, How to treat others, Love

PURPLE
Promises of God, Who I am in Christ

BROWN
Names, Times, Places, Locations, Numbers

Bible Study
Heealing & Hope

1. Isaiah 40:31
2. Philippians 1:6
3. Romans 15:13
4. Psalm 3:2-6
5. Jeremiah 29:11
6. 1 Peter 1:3-6
7. Philippians 3:13: -14
8. Romans 12:12
9. Pslam 27:13-14
10. Micah 7:5-7
11. Isaiah 30:18
12. Romans 15:4
13. 1 Peter 5:10
14. Pslam 123:1-2
15. Isaiah 43:1-2
16. Romans 8:18
17. 1 Corinthians 15:54-58
18. 1 John 3:2-3
19. Colossians 3:1-2
20. Hebrews 11:11
21. Psalm 147:11
22. Romans 8:28-29
23. Lamentations 3:25-26
24. Colossians 1:27
25. Romans 4:17-18
26. II Corinthians 4: 17-18
27. Proverbs 10:27-29
28. Psalm 62:5-6
29. Psalm 62:7-8
30. I Peter 3:14-15

Scripture_____

What is this scripture about?

What instruction, promise, wisdom or life principle did I learn from this scripture?

Scripture_____

What is this scripture about?

What instruction, promise, wisdom or life principle did I learn from this scripture?

Scripture_____

What is this scripture about?

What instruction, promise, wisdom or life principle did I learn from this scripture?

Scripture_____

What is this scripture about?

What instruction, promise, wisdom or life principle did I learn from this scripture?

Scripture_____

What is this scripture about?

What instruction, promise, wisdom or life principle did I learn from this scripture?

Scripture_____

What is this scripture about?

What instruction, promise, wisdom or life principle did I learn from this scripture?

Scripture_____

What is this scripture about?

What instruction, promise, wisdom or life principle did I learn from this scripture?

Scripture_____

What is this scripture about?

What instruction, promise, wisdom or life principle did I learn from this scripture?

Scripture_____

What is this scripture about?

What instruction, promise, wisdom or life principle did I learn from this scripture?

Scripture_____

What is this scripture about?

What instruction, promise, wisdom or life principle did I learn from this scripture?

Scripture_____

What is this scripture about?

What instruction, promise, wisdom or life principle did I learn from this scripture?

Scripture_____

What is this scripture about?

What instruction, promise, wisdom or life principle did I learn from this scripture?

Scripture_____

What is this scripture about?

What instruction, promise, wisdom or life principle did I learn from this scripture?

Scripture_____

What is this scripture about?

What instruction, promise, wisdom or life principle did I learn from this scripture?

Scripture_____

What is this scripture about?

What instruction, promise, wisdom or life principle did I learn from this scripture?

Scripture_____

What is this scripture about?

What instruction, promise, wisdom or life principle did I learn from this scripture?

Scripture_____

What is this scripture about?

What instruction, promise, wisdom or life principle did I learn from this scripture?

Scripture_____

What is this scripture about?

What instruction, promise, wisdom or life principle did I learn from this scripture?

Scripture_____

What is this scripture about?

What instruction, promise, wisdom or life principle did I learn from this scripture?

Scripture_____

What is this scripture about?

What instruction, promise, wisdom or life principle did I learn from this scripture?

Scripture_____

What is this scripture about?

What instruction, promise, wisdom or life principle did I learn from this scripture?

Scripture_____

What is this scripture about?

What instruction, promise, wisdom or life principle did I learn from this scripture?

Scripture_____

What is this scripture about?

What instruction, promise, wisdom or life principle did I learn from this scripture?

Scripture_____

What is this scripture about?

What instruction, promise, wisdom or life principle did I learn from this scripture?

Scripture_____

What is this scripture about?

What instruction, promise, wisdom or life principle did I learn from this scripture?

Scripture_____

What is this scripture about?

What instruction, promise, wisdom or life principle did I learn from this scripture?

Scripture_____

What is this scripture about?

What instruction, promise, wisdom or life principle did I learn from this scripture?

Scripture_____

What is this scripture about?

What instruction, promise, wisdom or life principle did I learn from this scripture?

Scripture_____

What is this scripture about?

What instruction, promise, wisdom or life principle did I learn from this scripture?

Scripture_____

What is this scripture about?

What instruction, promise, wisdom or life principle did I learn from this scripture?

Identity Study

Read this scripture and answer the correlating questions.

You did not choose me, but I chose you and appointed you so that you might go and bear fruit—fruit that will last—and so that whatever you ask in my name the Father will give you. This is my command: Love each other.
John 15:16-17

1. What is the truth associated with this scripture?

2. What does this scripture tell me about God?

3. What does this scripture say about me?

4. What lies has the enemy been feeding me about who I am? And what Bible verse could I use to combat against this?

Discerning God's Voice

Date-
___

Word or thought that passed through my head?

Is there a scripture that reflects this?

What does this thought mean to me, if anything?

Will it bring forth the Kingdom of God?

Will this bring forth good fruit?

___

Confirmation Checklist

☐ How?   ☐ How?   ☐ How?

Discerning God's Voice

Date- _____

Word or thought that passed through my head?

Is there a scripture that reflects this?

What does this thought mean to me, if anything?

Will it bring forth the Kingdom of God?

Will this bring forth good fruit?

Confirmation Checklist

☐ How?   ☐ How?   ☐ How?

Discerning God's Voice

Date-_____

Word or thought that passed through my head?

Is there a scripture that reflects this?

What does this thought mean to me, if anything?

Will it bring forth the Kingdom of God?

Will this bring forth good fruit?

_____

Confirmation Checklist

☐ How?   ☐ How?   ☐ How?

Obedience

What is God asking me to do?

Does this take me outside of my comfort zone?

Does it have the potential to be life changing for me or for someone else?

What would happen if I didn't do it?

What would happen if I did?

Final Outcome

Obedience

What is God asking me to do?

Does this take me outside of my comfort zone?

Does it have the potential to be life changing for me or for someone else?

What would happen if I didn't do it?

What would happen if I did?

Final Outcome

Prophecy Notes

Date:

Today's Note Worthy Events:

Correlating Scripture:

What do I think this means?

Prophecy Notes

Date:

Today's Note Worthy Events:

Correlating Scripture:

What do I think this means?

Prophecy Notes

Date:

Today's Note Worthy Events:

Correlating Scripture:

What do I think this means?

Rooted

month
───────────

Important Events

MONTH   **YEAR**

Sunday	Monday	Tuesday	Wednesday	Thursday	Friday	Saturday

MY NOTES

MY NOTES

MY NOTES

My Prayer Wall
"Prayer is Adventurous"

For Others:

[Y] Answered [N]

How has God answered or shifted this prayer?

For Myself:

[Y] Answered [N]

How has God answered or shifted this prayer?

My Prayer Wall
"Prayer is Adventurous"

For Others:

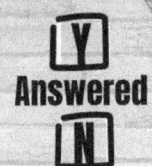

[Y] Answered
[N]

How has God answered or shifted this prayer?

For Myself:

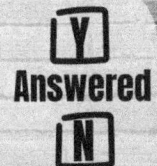

[Y] Answered
[N]

How has God answered or shifted this prayer?

My Prayer Wall
"Prayer is Adventurous"

For Others:

Answered: Y / N

How has God answered or shifted this prayer?

For Myself:

Answered: Y / N

How has God answered or shifted this prayer?

Prayer Challenges

Challenge 1 - Secret Prayer

This month I am praying for _____
Their specific needs are:

Date:

My Circle Prayer

Date:

My Circle Prayer

Date:

My Circle Prayer

> I have set my rainbow in the clouds, and it will be the sign of the covenant between me and the earth.   //Genesis 9:13

BIBLE Color Coding Guide

BLUE - Read through the entire passage again and underline all the names of God, Jesus, the Holy Spirit, and the Trinity in blue. Also underline the attributes of God and His character traits in blue as well.

GREEN - Read through the chapter or passage again, and this time search any commands, laws, or principles for life. Also look for references to obedience or spiritual growth and underline these mentions in green.

YELLOW - Then, read through the verses again and underline all references to eternity, heaven, or angels in yellow.

ORANGE - Use orange to underline references to sin, Satan, spiritual warfare, temptation, demons, or hell.

RED - Use red to highlight Christ, His work, prophecies regarding Christ or how He is foreshadowed in the Old Testament.

PINK - Identify relationships, love, or how to treat others and mark those in pink.

PURPLE - Use purple to mark who you are in Christ and the promises of God.

BROWN - Finally, read through the entire passage again and underline all names, times, places, locations, or numbers you come across in brown. It may be helpful to first look for proper nouns, such as 'Lazarus', and then search for times and numbers.

BLUE
Who God is, Names, Attributes

GREEN
Growth, Commands, Laws, Obedience, Fruitfulness

YELLOW
Eternity, Heaven, Angels, Hope

ORANGE
Sin, Satan, Spiritual Warfare, Temptation, Demons, or Hell

RED
Christ's atoning work, prophecy re: Christ, Christ seen in the Old Testament

PINK
Relationships, How to treat others, Love

PURPLE
Promises of God, Who I am in Christ

BROWN
Names, Times, Places, Locations, Numbers

Bible Study
Prayer

1. I John 5: 14-16
2. Hebrews 4:14-16
3. Jeremiah 29:12-13
4. Matthew 18:20
5. Mark 11:24-25
6. Matthew 6: 5-8
7. Matthew 6: 9-13
8. Psalm 18:6
9. Acts 16:25-26
10. I Timothy 2: 1-2, 8
11. Luke 18:1-8
12. Matthew 26:41
13. James 1:5-6
14. Philippians 4:6-7
15. John 14:13-14
16. Matthew 17:7-11
17. Proverbs 15:8
18. Ephesians 6:18
19. Ephesians 3:14-20
20. Romans 8:26-27
21. I John 1:9
22. Ephesians 1:15-20
23. Proverbs 15:29
24. James 5:13-20
25. I Thess 5:16-18
26. Psalm 145: 18
27. Matthew 5: 44-45
28. John 15:16
29. Luke 6:12
30. III John 1:2

Scripture_____

What is this scripture about?

What instruction, promise, wisdom or life principle did I learn from this scripture?

Scripture_____

What is this scripture about?

What instruction, promise, wisdom or life principle did I learn from this scripture?

Scripture_____

What is this scripture about?

What instruction, promise, wisdom or life principle did I learn from this scripture?

Scripture_____

What is this scripture about?

What instruction, promise, wisdom or life principle did I learn from this scripture?

Scripture_____

What is this scripture about?

What instruction, promise, wisdom or life principle did I learn from this scripture?

Scripture_____

What is this scripture about?

What instruction, promise, wisdom or life principle did I learn from this scripture?

Scripture_____

What is this scripture about?

What instruction, promise, wisdom or life principle did I learn from this scripture?

Scripture_____

What is this scripture about?

What instruction, promise, wisdom or life principle did I learn from this scripture?

Scripture_____

What is this scripture about?

What instruction, promise, wisdom or life principle did I learn from this scripture?

Scripture_____

What is this scripture about?

What instruction, promise, wisdom or life principle did I learn from this scripture?

Scripture_____

What is this scripture about?

What instruction, promise, wisdom or life principle did I learn from this scripture?

Scripture_____

What is this scripture about?

What instruction, promise, wisdom or life principle did I learn from this scripture?

Scripture_____

What is this scripture about?

What instruction, promise, wisdom or life principle did I learn from this scripture?

Scripture_____

What is this scripture about?

What instruction, promise, wisdom or life principle did I learn from this scripture?

Scripture_____

What is this scripture about?

What instruction, promise, wisdom or life principle did I learn from this scripture?

Scripture_____

What is this scripture about?

What instruction, promise, wisdom or life principle did I learn from this scripture?

Scripture_____

What is this scripture about?

What instruction, promise, wisdom or life principle did I learn from this scripture?

Scripture_____

What is this scripture about?

What instruction, promise, wisdom or life principle did I learn from this scripture?

Scripture_____

What is this scripture about?

What instruction, promise, wisdom or life principle did I learn from this scripture?

Scripture_____

What is this scripture about?

What instruction, promise, wisdom or life principle did I learn from this scripture?

Scripture_____

What is this scripture about?

What instruction, promise, wisdom or life principle did I learn from this scripture?

Scripture_____

What is this scripture about?

What instruction, promise, wisdom or life principle did I learn from this scripture?

Scripture_____

What is this scripture about?

What instruction, promise, wisdom or life principle did I learn from this scripture?

Scripture_____

What is this scripture about?

What instruction, promise, wisdom or life principle did I learn from this scripture?

Scripture_____

What is this scripture about?

What instruction, promise, wisdom or life principle did I learn from this scripture?

Scripture_____

What is this scripture about?

What instruction, promise, wisdom or life principle did I learn from this scripture?

Scripture_____

What is this scripture about?

What instruction, promise, wisdom or life principle did I learn from this scripture?

Scripture_____

What is this scripture about?

What instruction, promise, wisdom or life principle did I learn from this scripture?

Scripture_____

What is this scripture about?

What instruction, promise, wisdom or life principle did I learn from this scripture?

Scripture_____

What is this scripture about?

What instruction, promise, wisdom or life principle did I learn from this scripture?

Identity Study

Read this scripture and answer the correlating questions.

*So God created mankind in his own image,
in the image of God he created them; male and female he created them.
God blessed them and said to them, "Be fruitful and increase in number; fill
the earth and subdue it. Rule over the fish in the sea and the birds in the sky
and over every living creature that moves on the ground."*
Genesis 1:27-28

1. What is the truth associated with this scripture?

2. What does this scripture tell me about God?

3. What does this scripture say about me?

4. What lies has the enemy been feeding me about who I am? And what Bible verse could I use to combat against this?

Discerning God's Voice

Date-

Word or thought that passed through my head?

Is there a scripture that reflects this?

What does this thought mean to me, if anything?

Will it bring forth the Kingdom of God?

Will this bring forth good fruit?

Confirmation Checklist

☐ How? ☐ How? ☐ How?

Discerning God's Voice

Date-

Word or thought that passed through my head?

Is there a scripture that reflects this?

What does this thought mean to me, if anything?

Will it bring forth the Kingdom of God?

Will this bring forth good fruit?

Confirmation Checklist

☐ How?   ☐ How?   ☐ How?

Discerning God's Voice

Date-
_____

Word or thought that passed through my head?

Is there a scripture that reflects this?

What does this thought mean to me, if anything?

Will it bring forth the Kingdom of God?

Will this bring forth good fruit?

_____

Confirmation Checklist

☐ How? ☐ How? ☐ How?

Obedience

What is God asking me to do?

Does this take me outside of my comfort zone?

Does it have the potential to be life changing for me or for someone else?

What would happen if I didn't do it?

What would happen if I did?

Final Outcome

Obedience

What is God asking me to do?

Does this take me outside of my comfort zone?

Does it have the potential to be life changing for me or for someone else?

What would happen if I didn't do it?

What would happen if I did?

Final Outcome

Prophecy Notes

Date:

Today's Note Worthy Events:

Correlating Scripture:

What do I think this means?

Prophecy Notes

Date:

Today's Note Worthy Events:

Correlating Scripture:

What do I think this means?

Prophecy Notes

Date:

Today's Note Worthy Events:

Correlating Scripture:

What do I think this means?

Rooted

month
___

Important Events

MONTH　　　　　　　　　　　　　　　　　　**YEAR**

Sunday	Monday	Tuesday	Wednesday	Thursday	Friday	Saturday

MY NOTES

MY NOTES

MY NOTES

My Prayer Wall
"Prayer is Adventurous"

For Others:

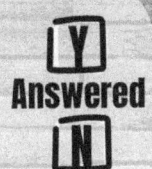

Answered [Y] [N]

How has God answered or shifted this prayer?

For Myself:

Answered [Y] [N]

How has God answered or shifted this prayer?

My Prayer Wall
"Prayer is Adventurous"

For Others:

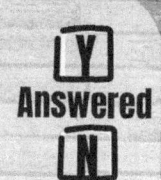

[Y] Answered
[N]

How has God answered or shifted this prayer?

For Myself:

[Y] Answered
[N]

How has God answered or shifted this prayer?

My Prayer Wall
"Prayer is Adventurous"

For Others:

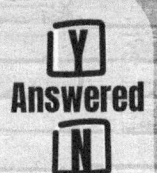

[Y] Answered [N]

How has God answered or shifted this prayer?

For Myself:

[Y] Answered [N]

How has God answered or shifted this prayer?

Prayer Challenges

Challenge 1 - Secret Prayer

This month I am praying for_____
Their specific needs are:

Date:

My Circle Prayer

Date:

My Circle Prayer

Date:

My Circle Prayer

> **I have set my rainbow in the clouds, and it will be the sign of the covenant between me and the earth.**   //*Genesis 9:13*

BIBLE
Color Coding Guide

BLUE - Read through the entire passage again and underline all the names of God, Jesus, the Holy Spirit, and the Trinity in blue. Also underline the attributes of God and His character traits in blue as well.

GREEN - Read through the chapter or passage again, and this time search any commands, laws, or principles for life. Also look for references to obedience or spiritual growth and underline these mentions in green.

YELLOW - Then, read through the verses again and underline all references to eternity, heaven, or angels in yellow.

ORANGE - Use orange to underline references to sin, Satan, spiritual warfare, temptation, demons, or hell.

RED - Use red to highlight Christ, His work, prophecies regarding Christ or how He is foreshadowed in the Old Testament.

PINK - Identify relationships, love, or how to treat others and mark those in pink.

PURPLE - Use purple to mark who you are in Christ and the promises of God.

BROWN - Finally, read through the entire passage again and underline all names, times, places, locations, or numbers you come across in brown. It may be helpful to first look for proper nouns, such as 'Lazarus', and then search for times and numbers.

BLUE
Who God is, Names, Attributes

GREEN
Growth, Commands, Laws, Obedience, Fruitfulness

YELLOW
Eternity, Heaven, Angels, Hope

ORANGE
Sin, Satan, Spiritual Warfare, Temptation, Demons, or Hell

RED
Christ's atoning work, prophecy re: Christ, Christ seen in the Old Testament

PINK
Relationships, How to treat others, Love

PURPLE
Promises of God, Who I am in Christ

BROWN
Names, Times, Places, Locations, Numbers

Bible Study
Repentance & Renewal

1. Acts 3:19-20
2. Zechariah 1:2-3
3. James 4:8-10
4. Joel 2:12-14
5. Revelation 2:1-7
6. Malachi 3:7-9
7. Isaiah 55:7
8. Jeremiah 24:7
9. 1 Peter 2:25
10. Jeremiah 2:1-2
11. Zechariah 8:2-3
12. Isaiah 1:18-20
13. 2 Corinthians 7:1
14. Hosea 14:1-2
15. 1 Peter 4:17
16. Ezekiel 5:5-8
17. Jeremiah 4:1-2
18. Jeremiah 29:13
19. Revelation 2:12-17
20. Hosea 6:1-3
21. Jeremiah 15:19
22. 1 Kings 18:21
23. Revelation 2:18-29
24. Isaiah 1:2-6
25. Psalm 51:12
26. Revelation 3:1-6
27. Isaiah 64:1-2
28. Isaiah 64:8-9
29. Revelation 3:14-22
30. Psalm 85:6

Scripture_____

What is this scripture about?

What instruction, promise, wisdom or life principle did I learn from this scripture?

Scripture_____

What is this scripture about?

What instruction, promise, wisdom or life principle did I learn from this scripture?

Scripture_____

What is this scripture about?

What instruction, promise, wisdom or life principle did I learn from this scripture?

Scripture_____

What is this scripture about?

What instruction, promise, wisdom or life principle did I learn from this scripture?

Scripture_____

What is this scripture about?

What instruction, promise, wisdom or life principle did I learn from this scripture?

Scripture_____

What is this scripture about?

What instruction, promise, wisdom or life principle did I learn from this scripture?

Scripture_____

What is this scripture about?

What instruction, promise, wisdom or life principle did I learn from this scripture?

Scripture_____

What is this scripture about?

What instruction, promise, wisdom or life principle did I learn from this scripture?

Scripture_____

What is this scripture about?

What instruction, promise, wisdom or life principle did I learn from this scripture?

Scripture_____

What is this scripture about?

What instruction, promise, wisdom or life principle did I learn from this scripture?

Scripture_____

What is this scripture about?

What instruction, promise, wisdom or life principle did I learn from this scripture?

Scripture_____

What is this scripture about?

What instruction, promise, wisdom or life principle did I learn from this scripture?

Scripture_____

What is this scripture about?

What instruction, promise, wisdom or life principle did I learn from this scripture?

Scripture_____

What is this scripture about?

What instruction, promise, wisdom or life principle did I learn from this scripture?

Scripture_____

What is this scripture about?

What instruction, promise, wisdom or life principle did I learn from this scripture?

Scripture_____

What is this scripture about?

What instruction, promise, wisdom or life principle did I learn from this scripture?

Scripture_____

What is this scripture about?

What instruction, promise, wisdom or life principle did I learn from this scripture?

Scripture_____

What is this scripture about?

What instruction, promise, wisdom or life principle did I learn from this scripture?

Scripture_____

What is this scripture about?

What instruction, promise, wisdom or life principle did I learn from this scripture?

Scripture_____

What is this scripture about?

What instruction, promise, wisdom or life principle did I learn from this scripture?

Scripture_____

What is this scripture about?

What instruction, promise, wisdom or life principle did I learn from this scripture?

Scripture_____

What is this scripture about?

What instruction, promise, wisdom or life principle did I learn from this scripture?

Scripture_____

What is this scripture about?

What instruction, promise, wisdom or life principle did I learn from this scripture?

Scripture_____

What is this scripture about?

What instruction, promise, wisdom or life principle did I learn from this scripture?

Scripture_____

What is this scripture about?

What instruction, promise, wisdom or life principle did I learn from this scripture?

Scripture_____

What is this scripture about?

What instruction, promise, wisdom or life principle did I learn from this scripture?

Scripture_____

What is this scripture about?

What instruction, promise, wisdom or life principle did I learn from this scripture?

Scripture_____

What is this scripture about?

What instruction, promise, wisdom or life principle did I learn from this scripture?

Scripture_____

What is this scripture about?

What instruction, promise, wisdom or life principle did I learn from this scripture?

Scripture_____

What is this scripture about?

What instruction, promise, wisdom or life principle did I learn from this scripture?

Identity Study

Read this scripture and answer the correlating questions.

But you are a chosen people, a royal priesthood, a holy nation, God's special possession, that you may declare the praises of him who called you out of darkness into his wonderful light.
Peter2:9

1. What is the truth associated with this scripture?

2. What does this scripture tell me about God?

3. What does this scripture say about me?

4. What lies has the enemy been feeding me about who I am? And what Bible verse could I use to combat against this?

Discerning God's Voice

Date-

Word or thought that passed through my head?

Is there a scripture that reflects this?

What does this thought mean to me, if anything?

Will it bring forth the Kingdom of God?

Will this bring forth good fruit?

Confirmation Checklist

☐ How?   ☐ How?   ☐ How?

Discerning God's Voice

Date-

Word or thought that passed through my head?

Is there a scripture that reflects this?

What does this thought mean to me, if anything?

Will it bring forth the Kingdom of God?

Will this bring forth good fruit?

Confirmation Checklist

☐ How?   ☐ How?   ☐ How?

Discerning God's Voice

Date-

Word or thought that passed through my head?

Is there a scripture that reflects this?

What does this thought mean to me, if anything?

Will it bring forth the Kingdom of God?

Will this bring forth good fruit?

Confirmation Checklist

☐ How? ☐ How? ☐ How?

Obedience

What is God asking me to do?

Does this take me outside of my comfort zone?

Does it have the potential to be life changing for me or for someone else?

What would happen if I didn't do it?

What would happen if I did?

Final Outcome

Obedience

What is God asking me to do?

Does this take me outside of my comfort zone?

Does it have the potential to be life changing for me or for someone else?

What would happen if I didn't do it?

What would happen if i did?

Final Outcome

Prophecy Notes

Date:

Today's Note Worthy Events:

Correlating Scripture:

What do I think this means?

Stacy Renee is a wife and mother to two incredible boys. Throughout her entrepreneurial journey, she has successfully established and managed various businesses, ranging from Real Estate to Photography. Her deep devotion to Jesus and the transformative journey of following Him has led her to initiate the Rooted 4 Jesus movement. This endeavor aims to spread the teachings of the Word to all corners of the world.
"People often have questions about faith, and that's completely normal," Stacy shares. "Even the most ardent followers of Jesus grapple with uncertainties." Through her experiences, she has realized the significance of intentionality and fostering a supportive community. To aid others on this spiritual journey she has created this journal.

In addition to her entrepreneurial ventures, Stacy also runs a successful ministry that encompasses online evangelism, women's conferences, and authorship of Bible studies, devotionals, and journals. After trying numerous journals, Stacy felt overwhelmed and unsure where to begin. She sought a tool that could offer guidance, spark adventure, be enjoyable, and yet challenge her. The journal creation process felt divinely inspired, taking only two weeks to come to fruition. Stacy hopes others will find as much joy in using the journal as she does.

Stacy and her family uprooted their entire lives in 2016 and moved from Michigan to California to help plant a church in the Bay area. The most unchurched, de-churched area in the USA. " When we left MI, my husband wasn't even a true follower of Jesus, but through our journey God showed up in a mighty way and has turned our entire family around and grown our faith immeasurably.